DATE DUE

JUN.09.1995	JUL.07.1993		
JUN.22.1995	SEP.15.1998		
AUG.08.1995	OCT.13.1998		
OCT.10.1995	DEC.09.1998		
MAR26.1996	MAR12.1999		
JUL.18.1996	APR.02.1999		
SEP.17.1996	JUL.16.1999		
OCT.17.1997			
NOV.18.1997	MAY18.2000		
FEB.13.1998			

Demco, Inc. 38-293

TECHNOLOGY CRAFT TOPICS

HOUSES and HOMES

Chris Oxlade

illustrated by **Raymond Turvey**

photography by **Martyn Chillmaid**

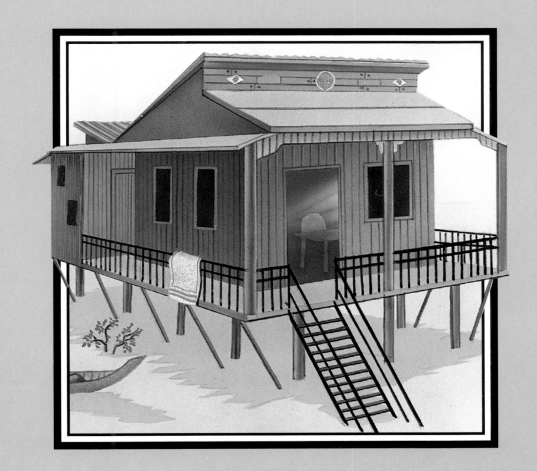

FRANKLIN WATTS
New York ▪ Chicago ▪ London ▪ Toronto ▪ Sydney

Warning!

Be very careful when cutting with sharp equipment. To cut the materials used in the projects, you will need scissors, a craft knife, and a small handsaw. Remember, always use a board when cutting with a knife or saw.

© Franklin Watts 1994

Franklin Watts
95 Madison Avenue
New York, NY 10016

10 9 8 7 6 5 4 3 2 1

Library of Congress Cataloging-in-Publication Data

Oxlade. Chris
    Houses and homes / by Chris Oxlade.
    p. cm.— (Technology craft topics)
    Includes index.
    ISBN 0-531-14330-9 (lib. bdg.)
    1. House construction — History — Juvenile literature. 2. Model
houses — Juvenile literature. [1. House construction.] I. Title.
II. Series: Technology craft topics.
TH4808.093 1994
690' .837 — dc20   94-15514
                                           CIP AC

Series editor: Belinda Weber
Editor: Jane Walker
Designer: Glynn Pickerill
Illustrator: Raymond Turvey
Design production: The R & B Partnership
Cover design and artwork: Mike Davis
Photography: Martyn Chillmaid
Consultant: Rowland Penfold

Printed in the United Kingdom

CONTENTS

HOUSES and HOMES

You might not think that houses and homes have much to do with technology. Yet even prehistoric people used technology to build their primitive homes. Technology involves the use of available materials and skills to provide people with the things they need. These early people used simple building methods and basic materials such as animal skins and bones. Modern houses have many technological features such as central heating and double glazed windows. Although there are many different styles of homes, they all provide shelter for people.

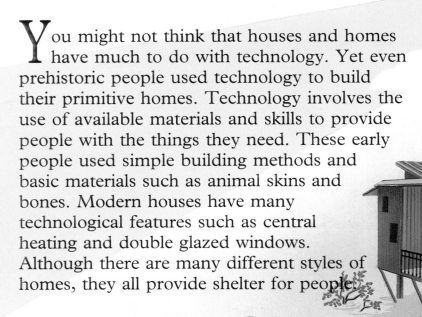

In Southeast Asia, many people live on the banks of massive rivers, such as the Mekong, which flows down from the mountains around Tibet. Some live in houses on stilts (right), so these homes are not flooded when the rivers burst their banks during the monsoon season.

Most houses around the world are built using materials that are found locally. For example, houses in areas where there are large forests are often built completely of wood.

Modern building materials, such as concrete and steel, are used to build huge apartment buildings. High-rises like this are one way to provide lots of homes (and offices) in crowded city centers.

Brick is a building material that has been used for thousands of years. In hot countries, bricks can be made simply by drying blocks of mud in the sun. House bricks are made by baking blocks of clay in an oven (above). The color of the brick depends on the color of the clay.

In some parts of the world, people called nomads wander from place to place. They need portable homes that can easily be packed away and carried to another site. Mongolian nomads live in a type of tent called a yurt (below). It has a wooden frame covered with layers of felt and canvas.

Houses protect people from the weather – from the heat and the cold as well as the rain and wind. In very hot countries, buildings are painted in light colors so that the sun's rays are reflected away from them. This helps to keep the inside of the houses cool.

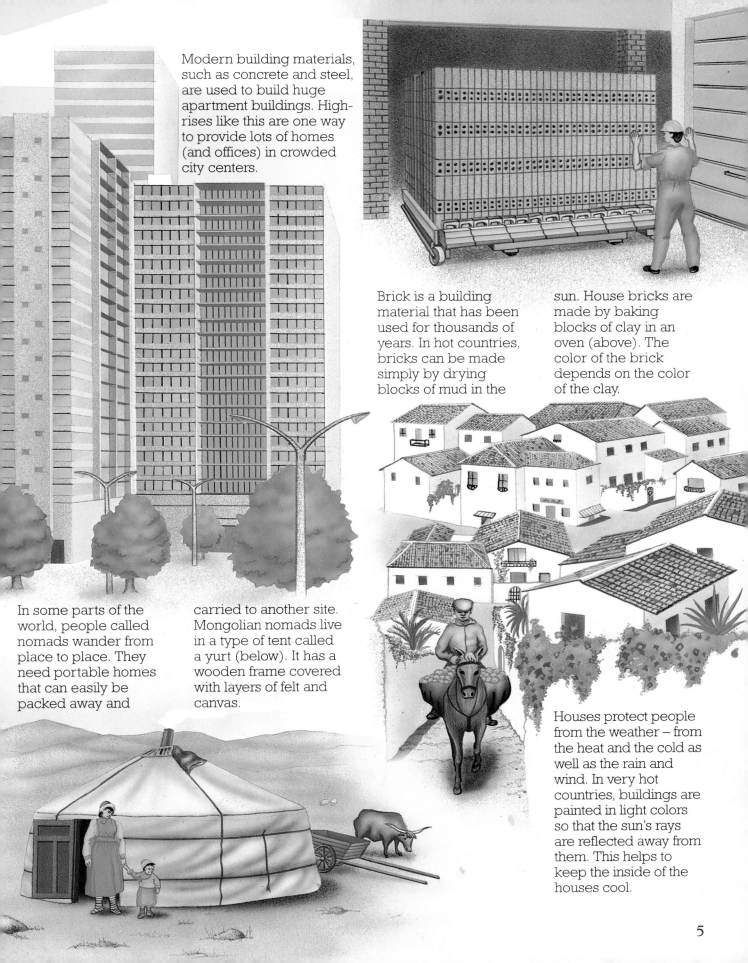

HISTORY of HOUSES and HOMES

Houses and homes have a history that is as long as the history of people themselves. Some early peoples sheltered in caves. Later they built simple huts. Permanent homes developed when the first villages and cities appeared – from about 9,000 B.C. New materials and building methods gradually developed as homes became more elaborate. For example, stone and brick walls mostly replaced wooden frames. However, in some countries, houses and homes have stayed the same for hundreds of years.

The first homes

The very first homes were simple temporary shelters. They were made from branches that were bent together to form dome-shaped huts. Evidence of these huts has been found in modern-day Tanzania. They were built by prehistoric people two million years ago. Simple homes like these were still being built about 12,000 years ago by some hunter-gatherers (above). These people moved around the countryside hunting animals and collecting plants for food. The animals they caught also provided them with building materials, such as hides (skins) and bones.

Homes began to change when people began to settle down. When people stayed in the same place to plant and harvest their crops, villages began to grow. In the Far East, houses were built with mud bricks covered in plaster. They had a main room and smaller side rooms. Inside were ovens, benches, and storage places. Around 5000 B.C., people in Europe built long huts called longhouses (left). They had timber frames, mud walls, and straw roofs.

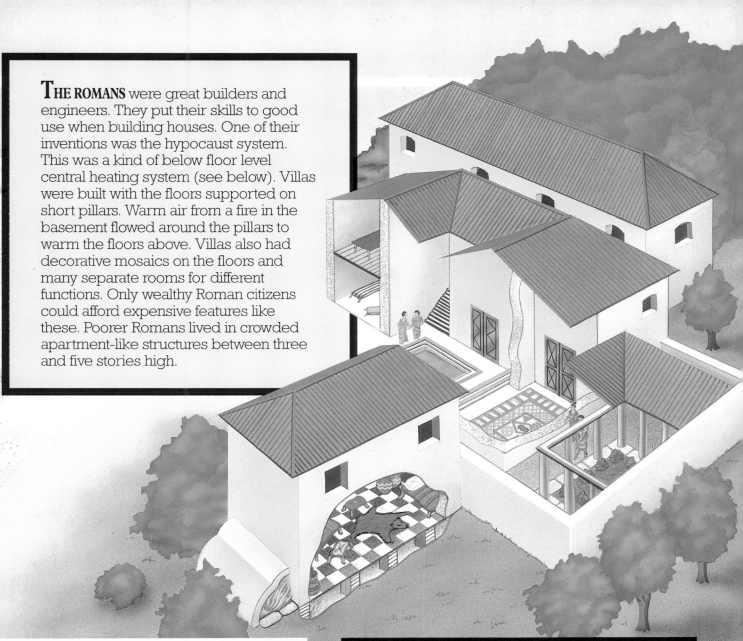

THE ROMANS were great builders and engineers. They put their skills to good use when building houses. One of their inventions was the hypocaust system. This was a kind of below floor level central heating system (see below). Villas were built with the floors supported on short pillars. Warm air from a fire in the basement flowed around the pillars to warm the floors above. Villas also had decorative mosaics on the floors and many separate rooms for different functions. Only wealthy Roman citizens could afford expensive features like these. Poorer Romans lived in crowded apartment-like structures between three and five stories high.

IN THE MIDDLE AGES, the main method of house building in Europe was to construct a timber frame and fill the gaps with a mixture of sticks and mud, called wattle and daub. In the late seventeenth century, stone and brick began to be used to build house walls. These walls supported the floors and the roof. During the Industrial Revolution, thousands of workers' cottages were constructed in Great Britain. Most, like these terraced houses in Skipton, England (left), were made from stone and brick.

Making a model TIMBER-FRAMED HUT

Timber-framed huts were the most common type of home in Europe for thousands of years. The main reason was the existence of huge areas of forest to supply building materials. A typical hut had a timber frame made of tree trunks and thick branches. The side walls were made from wattle and daub. The roof was thatched with bundles of straw or reeds.

To make a timber-framed hut

You may need:

- **plywood or thick cardboard (at least 12 in x 8 in/30 cm x 20 cm)**
- **wooden dowels**
- **cardboard**
- **popsicle sticks**
- **twigs**
- **strips of wood**
- **a small handsaw**
- **modeling clay**
- **bundles of straw or strips of paper**
- **paper drinking straws**
- **string**
- **glue**
- **paints**
- **a paintbrush**

1 Before you start building, plan your hut. The main thing to decide is the shape of the frame and how it will be joined together. When you have designed your hut, mark the positions for the posts on the plywood or cardboard.

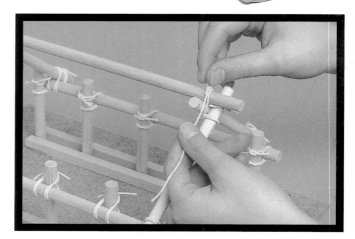

2 Now construct your timber frame. Carefully cut lengths of dowel or twigs for the posts and beams. Join the frame together by wrapping string around the joints. The posts in a full-size hut would be buried in deep post holes. Keep your posts upright on the plywood by gluing strips of wood next to them or by using modeling clay.

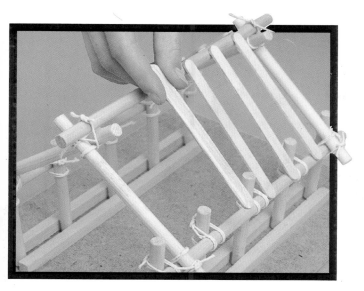

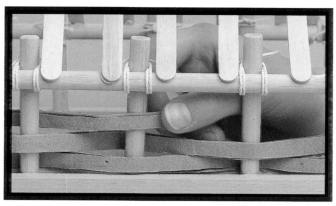

3 Use popsicle sticks for the roof. These will hold up the thatch when you add it. Make a grid pattern by adding sticks up and down the roof and across it.

4 Now make the walls. Weave straws or narrow strips of cardboard in and out of the poles along each side. Start at the bottom and work your way to the top. Cut off any bits of straw that stick out.

5 Finally, add the thatched roof. Gather together small bundles of straw. Tie up the bundles with string and cut them to the right length for your roof. Tie them to the main roof beam. Use some glue to keep them in the right place.

Did You Know...

... that archaeologists can only guess what the timber-framed huts of long ago looked like? Unlike mud and stone buildings that survive for many years, timber ones quickly rot. All that's left of a timber-framed hut is usually the post holes, with rotting wood inside.

The only parts missing from the hut are the walls at each end. These might have been made from logs that were placed on end. Use twigs to add end walls to your hut. Remember to leave a doorway.

Try painting the plywood to look like the ground around a hut. You could include a muddy patch by the door.

AROUND the WORLD

A great variety of different house styles can be found around the world. Why are they so different? One of the reasons for these differences is the local materials available to builders. Another reason is that houses are designed to protect people against the climate of a particular country. In some places, although new materials are available, houses are still built in the traditional style because traditional materials are cheaper.

Town houses

In England, millions of people live in town and city suburbs. Most of their houses have been built in the twentieth century. They all have services supplied directly to the house – water, gas, and electricity. The houses are designed to keep out the wind and rain and keep in the heat. The sloping roofs allow rainwater to run down into the gutters before it has a chance to get through the roof. Most houses have cavity walls. These are walls that consist of two layers with a gap in between. The gap keeps water from getting into the house as well as heat from getting out.

IN THE RAIN FORESTS of South America, many Indian tribes still live as they have for thousands of years. They use the resources of the forest around them for all their needs. The Indians make building frames for their houses (above) from saplings held together with vines. Roofs and walls are made from large, broad palm leaves or they are thatched with dried grass.

Homes in cold places

People living in very cold parts of the world need specially adapted homes to keep them warm, even in the harshest weather. They have solved the problem in different ways. In Scandinavia, permanent houses like the one shown at left have special features to keep in the warmth. They are very well insulated and have triple glazing to stop heat from getting out through the windows. In the Arctic, some Lapps (who live in the far north of Scandinavia) need temporary homes when out hunting. Traditional Lapp tents (below) have stick floors covered in reindeer skins to keep out the cold from the frozen ground. A fire in the middle of the tent keeps the people warm.

TALL REEDS that grow along the banks of rivers and lakes make good building materials. Houses are still built from reeds in some parts of the world. Reeds from Lake Titicaca, in South America, are woven together into mats that are used as wall panels for houses (left). Marsh Arabs, who live in the marshlands between the Tigris and Euphrates rivers in Iraq, also build reed houses. Reed mats are attached to a frame made of reed bundles. The houses are built on artificial islands in the marshes. Reeds are also used for thatching the roofs of houses in other areas of the world.

Making a REED HOUSE

Reed is used as building material in many parts of the world – in fact, wherever it grows. The houses of the Marsh Arabs of Iraq are built completely of reed. The Marsh Arabs make reed into bundles and mats. The bundles form the structure of the house and the mats make up the walls and roof.

To make a model reed house
You may need:

- straw
- old manila envelopes
- corrugated cardboard
- thick cardboard or posterboard baseboard
- string
- a craft knife
- glue
- paints

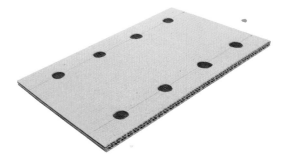

1 Draw a rectangular shape (about 12 in x 8 in/30 cm x 20 cm) on your baseboard to show the outline of the reed house. The roof and walls will be supported by arches, one at each end and two or three spaced out in between. Mark the positions of the arches on the baseboard.

2 Now make the arches. Gather together bundles of straw and tie them with string. Trim the ends so that each bundle is long enough to make an arch. Make enough bundles for all the arches. Instead of straw, you can bundle together thin strips of corrugated cardboard.

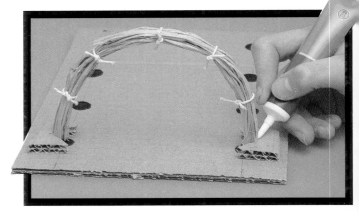

3 Cut out small pieces of corrugated cardboard and cut a V shape along one side of each piece. Glue the pieces onto the baseboard where the feet of the arches are marked. Bend one straw bundle over and glue its feet in place. Glue the other bundles onto the baseboard in the same way.

4 Make several long thin bundles of straw. Tie them along the sides and across the top to complete the house frame.

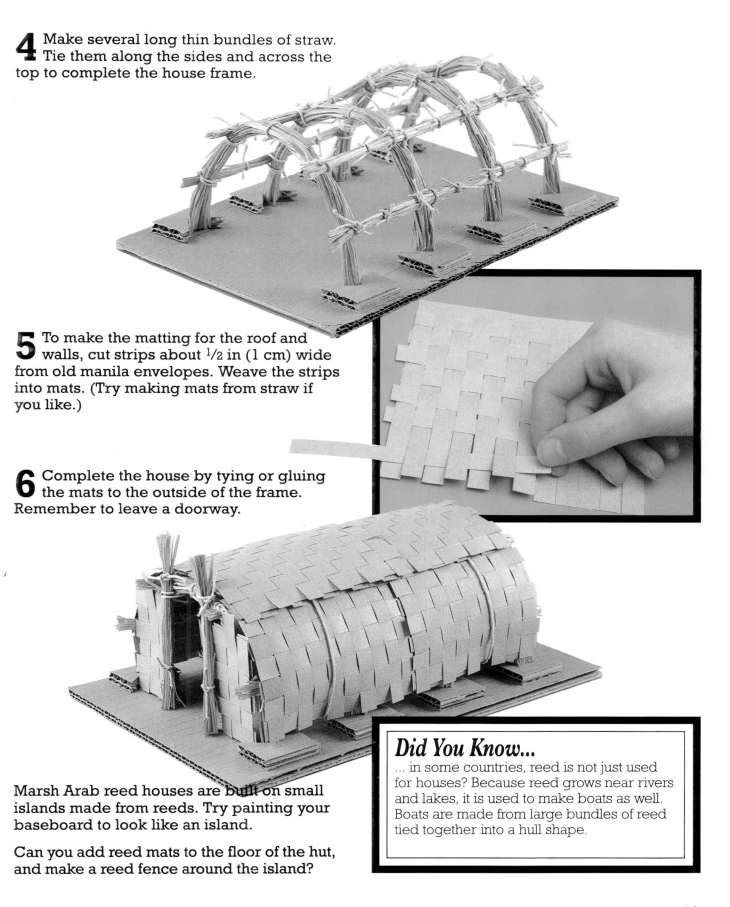

5 To make the matting for the roof and walls, cut strips about 1/2 in (1 cm) wide from old manila envelopes. Weave the strips into mats. (Try making mats from straw if you like.)

6 Complete the house by tying or gluing the mats to the outside of the frame. Remember to leave a doorway.

Marsh Arab reed houses are built on small islands made from reeds. Try painting your baseboard to look like an island.

Can you add reed mats to the floor of the hut, and make a reed fence around the island?

Did You Know...

... in some countries, reed is not just used for houses? Because reed grows near rivers and lakes, it is used to make boats as well. Boats are made from large bundles of reed tied together into a hull shape.

HOMES on the Move

The first homes that the early peoples built were temporary shelters. They were used by hunter-gatherers who moved from place to place in search of food. Many people around the world still live in this way. In the Kalahari Desert in southern Africa, San bushmen carry huts of sticks and grass with them for shelter at night. Other people use tents and caravans for temporary homes while they are traveling.

CARAVANS ARE HOMES on wheels. They were originally built and used by gypsies. Gypsies are descended from nomadic people who originally came from India. Some gypsies still live in traditional wooden, horse-drawn caravans (left). Conditions inside the caravans are cramped, but the interior is well planned, with a place for everything. Caravans were also used by traveling traders and players. Caravans evolved into modern-day trailers and are often very sophisticated. Many have hot and cold running water and a toilet. Some even have central heating. Trailers are a good example of space-saving design. A mobile home is a small truck with a trailer-like interior.

Tents

A tent is a shelter made from fabric. The fabric is normally held up by poles and ropes. Many people around the world still live in tents. They are mainly nomads, who move from place to place hunting or trading livestock. Their tents are easy to put up and take down, and are often carried on the backs of their animals. Bedouins trade camels, goats, and sheep in the deserts of the Middle East. Their traditional tents (above) are made from woven goat-hair cloth stretched over poles. The tents keep them cool in the very hot daytime and warm in the nights, which can be very cold. Inside their tents, the Bedouins sit on carpets and cushions.

Today, tents are widely used by people on vacation. Modern tents like the one above are made from waterproof synthetic fabrics, like nylon. Some large tents are like small houses. They have a covered entryway and two or three rooms inside. The tent material is held up by poles. The poles are held steady by ropes called guy ropes. The whole tent can usually be packed away into a small trailer. Special tents are made for mountaineers (left). These tents are designed to be quickly erected, waterproof, and wind-resistant. They are able to be packed into a small bag, and are lightweight enough to be carried.

Making a Model
NOMAD TENT

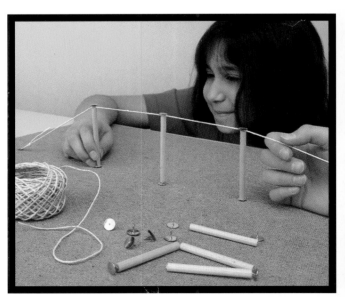

The picture on page 15 shows a tent built by the Bedouin nomads who live in the deserts of the Middle East. Can you see how the tent is held up? You can make a model Bedouin tent that works in the same way. A cloth roof and cloth walls are supported by poles held up by guy ropes.

To make a Bedouin tent

You may need:

- plywood baseboard
- thin wooden dowels
- twigs
- string
- thumbtacks
- scraps of fabric
- modeling clay
- scissors
- a handsaw

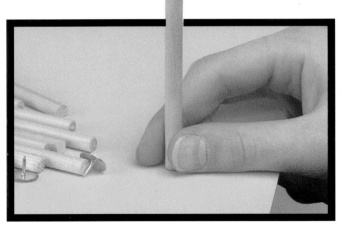

1 First, you need to make the tent poles: three tall ones to support the center of the tent and six shorter ones, three down each side. Cut the lengths from thin dowels or twigs. Push a thumbtack into the top of each pole, but not all the way in. Leave a gap between the top of the pole and the head of the thumbtack.

2 Push a thumbtack into the baseboard in the center along one side. Cut a piece of string about 8 in (20 cm) longer than the baseboard and tie one end to the thumbtack. Place the three long poles in a row across the center of the baseboard. Use modeling clay on the bottom of the poles to hold them in place.

3 Ask a friend to hold the long poles steady while you stretch the string around the thumbtacks on their tops and around another thumbtack on the baseboard.

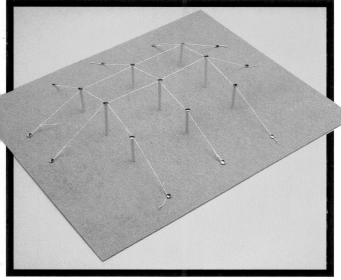

4 Now put up the side poles in the same way. This time, stretch the string across the baseboard and wrap it around the center poles on the way. You should end up with a firm structure of poles and ropes.

5 Cut three panels of fabric to make the end walls and the inside wall of the tent. Fold the fabric over the ropes that run across the tent. Make the panels large enough so that the bottom of each one drags on the ground.

6 Now measure the size of your tent. Add ³/₄ in (2 cm) to the length to work out how big the roof needs to be. Cut the roof from a piece of fabric. Lay it over the top of the tent so that it hangs over the ends slightly.

Can you figure out a way to attach the roof to the poles so that it wont blow off? Try making carpets and cushions to fit inside the tent.

How easy is it to take down and put up your tent? Could you make any improvements to your design to speed up the process?

Bedouins pack their tents into bundles that are carried by camels. Try packing your tent into a neat bundle.

FORTIFIED HOMES

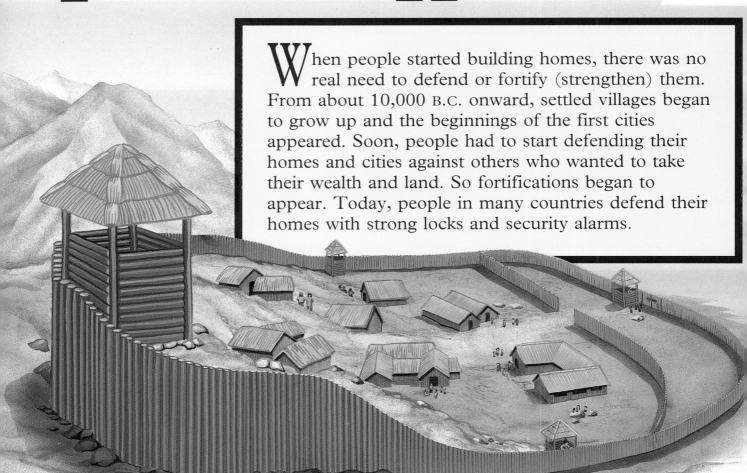

When people started building homes, there was no real need to defend or fortify (strengthen) them. From about 10,000 B.C. onward, settled villages began to grow up and the beginnings of the first cities appeared. Soon, people had to start defending their homes and cities against others who wanted to take their wealth and land. So fortifications began to appear. Today, people in many countries defend their homes with strong locks and security alarms.

THE FIRST FORTIFIED TOWNS and cities appeared around the Mediterranean Sea from about 6000 B.C. onward. The rulers of these cities became rich through trading. They had to defend their wealth, and so large defensive stone walls were built around the cities. In northern Europe, villages began to have defensive wooden walls built around them to protect them from attack. Towers along the walls were used as lookout posts. The village shown above dates from around 1000 B.C.

Carcassonne in Southwest France (above) is one of the best-preserved examples of a medieval walled town.

Castles and keeps

In Europe, from the eleventh century onward, kings and nobles protected themselves and their wealth inside fortified homes. The greatest fortified homes were castles. A castle was both a military fort and a home for the lord, his family, his servants, and followers. Many castles were almost self-sufficient in food and materials – almost like small, self-contained towns.

Castles were carefully designed so that they were difficult to attack and easy to defend. The site was chosen carefully. A hilltop with clear views over the surrounding land was the most attractive. A well-designed castle could defend itself against enemy soldiers for many months on end.

Larger castles had a ditch, or moat, around the outside. It was often filled with water. Then came an outer wall, with another line of defense inside it – a building called the keep. There was only one entrance through the outer wall. It was overlooked by towers, making an attack almost impossible.

CASTLES BECAME less important after medieval times. Military defenses were still built, but they were no longer used as homes. Today, we have no need to fortify our homes against enemy soldiers, but home security is still very important. Strong locks on doors and windows prevent burglars and intruders from entering our homes. Many homes also have an alarm system that shrills if a door or window is opened. The alarm can only be turned on and off by a person who knows the system's special code.

Building a CASTLE TOWER

Large medieval castles were designed to be easily defended. They had a central tower called the keep. This was where the lord and his family had their living and sleeping quarters. The keep was like a small castle with its own defenses. Around the outside of the castle grounds was a high wall called a curtain wall. Towers were built at regular intervals in the curtain wall. They provided good lookout points and also allowed defenders to see along the outside of the curtain wall.

To make a castle tower

You may need:

- corrugated cardboard
- thick cardboard as a baseboard
- thin cardboard
- glue
- popsicle sticks
- colored construction paper
- paints
- a craft knife
- a ruler

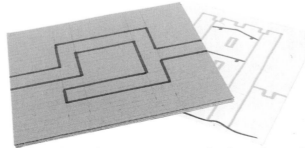

1 Draw a plan of your tower on the baseboard. A 5 in x 5 in (12 cm x 12 cm) square is a good size. Decide how many floors you want, where the curtain wall will join to the tower, and where to position arrow slots.

2 Using a craft knife with the help of an adult, carefully cut some thick corrugated cardboard into strips, about 3/4 in (2 cm) wide. You could use old cardboard boxes.

20

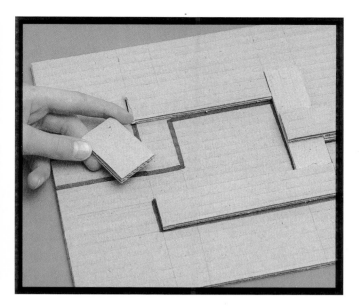

3 Build up the tower walls layer by layer. Cut pieces from the cardboard strips and glue them on top of each other. Remember to leave a doorway from the bottom level out into the castle courtyard. Leave out a section of wall to make a hole so that you can see inside the tower.

4 When you reach the level of the first floor, add some supports to hold up the floor. Make a floor from popsicle sticks. Now build the walls of the next level. Leave doorways out to the walkways on the curtain wall. Also, make arrow slots in the walls.

5 At the top of the tower, add a walkway and wall. The wall should have slots in it where defenders can shoot their arrows. Add a roof over the center of the tower to cover the floor below.

6 Paint the baseboard around the tower to look like the ground, or cover the area with green construction paper.

Did You Know...

... that spiral staircases in castles wound around clockwise as they went upward? This was so that a right-handed castle defender could swing his sword easily at an attacker lower down the staircase.

Can you extend the curtain wall by adding plywood at the sides? Try adding wooden buildings on the inside of the wall. These were used for stables and storage.

HIGH-TECH HOUSES

Houses today are built with special materials and construction methods to make sure that they are safe and secure to live in, and cheap and efficient to heat. In cold climates, it is important that a house keeps in the warmth from the heating system. This helps to reduce the cost of heating the house, and also helps to conserve precious fuel supplies. Heat is saved by insulating the walls, doors, windows, and roof of a house (right). Building regulations say what kinds of materials must be used for houses, to stop fire from spreading too quickly, for example.

INSULATION KEEPS a house warm by slowing down the rate at which heat from the inside escapes to the outside. Heat escapes from all over a house – through walls, windows, doors, floors, and the roof. Insulators are materials that do not let heat pass through them quickly. Good insulating materials are those which trap air to stop it from circulating and carrying away the heat. Roofs and floors can be insulated with a thick material made from glass fiber. Double and triple glazed windows trap a layer of air between the panes of glass. Walls with a cavity in the middle can be insulated by injecting foam into the cavity. It is also important to stop drafts around doors and windows. However, it is also necessary to allow some air to flow through a house. This ventilation will keep it free from dampness.

Energy from the sun

All energy comes to the earth from the sun. We call it solar energy. Houses in some countries are specially adapted to collect solar energy. They use it to heat water and also to heat the air inside the house (right). Solar energy saves on the use of other forms of energy. Water can be heated by solar panels, which are usually put on the roof of the house. The panels have pipes running through them, and the water in the pipes warms up. In hot countries, solar panels can heat nearly all the hot water needed by a family.

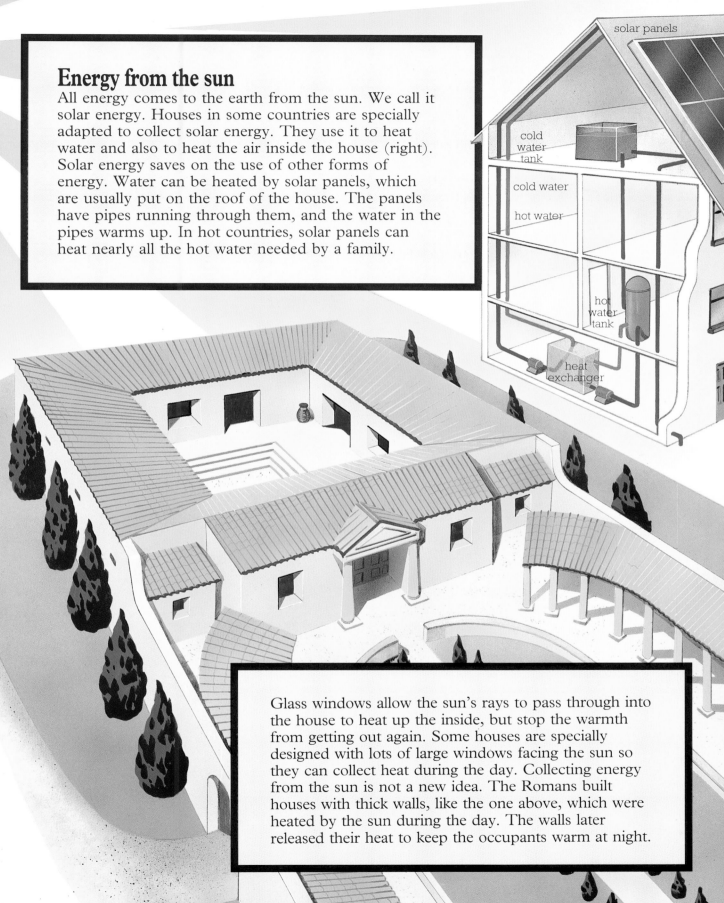

solar panels

cold water tank

cold water

hot water

hot water tank

heat exchanger

Glass windows allow the sun's rays to pass through into the house to heat up the inside, but stop the warmth from getting out again. Some houses are specially designed with lots of large windows facing the sun so they can collect heat during the day. Collecting energy from the sun is not a new idea. The Romans built houses with thick walls, like the one above, which were heated by the sun during the day. The walls later released their heat to keep the occupants warm at night.

Building a
SOLAR WATER HEATER

A solar water heater collects the sun's rays and uses their energy to heat up water for washing and heating. A complete solar heating system consists of a collector to catch the energy and warm the water, pipes to carry cold water to the collector and warm water away from it, and tanks to hold the warm water until it is needed. You can make a simple solar heater with all these parts.

To make a solar water heater
You may need:

- plastic tubing (about 16½ feet/5 m)
- plywood or thick cardboard as a baseboard
- strips of wood
- black construction paper
- flat black paint
- plastic soda bottles
- plastic wrap
- double-sided tape
- transparent tape
- glue
- scissors
- clothespins

2 The inside of the solar panel needs to be as dark as possible. This is because dark colors collect, or absorb, heat better than light colors. Paint the baseboard and the walls with flat black paint, or glue black construction paper onto the base and the walls.

1 Cut out a piece of plywood or thick cardboard for a baseboard. You need a piece about 12 in (30 cm) square. Cut strips of wood to make walls around the sides of the board. Glue the strips to the baseboard. Leave two gaps in the wall, one for the pipe to enter and the other for it to leave.

3 Lay the tubing across the baseboard so that about 29½ feet (75 cm) stick out through one of the gaps in the wall. Now curl the tubing in a spiral toward the middle. When about 3 feet (1 m) of tubing is left, lay it across the spiral and out of the other gap in the wall. Put strips of double-sided tape on the board to keep the tubing in place.

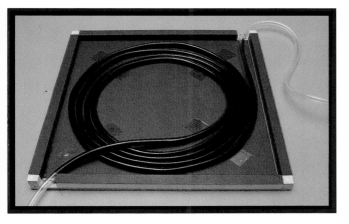

4 Paint the top side of the tubing black. When the paint is dry, lay a large piece of plastic wrap on top of the tubing. Wrap it over the walls and around the back of the board. Secure it down at the back with tape.

Did You Know...

... that there is a solar power plant in the Pyrenees Mountains in France? A huge set of mirrors reflects the sunlight and concentrates it onto a special collector called a furnace. The temperature inside the furnace reaches 5,432°F (3,000°C).

5 Prop the collector up on a chair or window-sill in the sunshine. Carefully cut the tops off two plastic soda bottles. Put one plastic bottle filled with water next to the collector. Feed one of the ends of the tubing into the bottle. Put an empty bottle on the floor below your collector. Fold over the free end of the tube and secure it with a clothespin. This stops the water from flowing through the tubing too fast.

6 Suck the free end of the tubing so that the water begins to flow through it. If the water flow is very slow, remove the clothespin and suck again. When the water is flowing, put the end of the tubing into the empty bottle. The empty bottle must be at a lower level than the full one. The water should drip through gradually.

Does the water dripping from your solar heater feel warmer than the water going in? How much warmer? Can you measure it with a thermometer?

What difference does it make to the flow of the water if you adjust the clothespin?

HIGH-RISE HOMES

Millions of people in towns and cities across the world live in multistory apartment buildings. High-rise buildings are a common way of providing large numbers of homes in crowded cities where land is scarce. Building an apartment building is much more complicated than building individual houses. Huge foundations are needed. There must be space for staircases, elevator shafts, and services, like water pipes. Safety is very important, too, especially in the event of fire.

These strange-looking "skyscrapers" are found in Cappadocia, in central Turkey. They were hacked out of soft volcanic rocks by Christian hermits long ago. Whole villages were created in this way. Today these buildings are still used by local farmers.

HIGH-RISE HOMES are not a new idea. In large Roman cities, poor people lived in types of apartments called *insulae*. The ground floor was usually occupied by stores. The apartments had no kitchens or toilets. In Yemen, people have built and lived in multistory houses made from mud bricks (left) for more than one thousand years. The houses are up to ten stories high and built very close together. The walls are thicker at the bottom to handle the weight from above. Apartment buildings like these, where facilities such as bathrooms and cooking are shared, are called tenements.

Building a skyscraper

The first skyscrapers were built in the United States in the late nineteenth century, when engineers invented iron and steel frameworks to support these buildings. Until that time, buildings could only be a few stories high because the supporting stone or brickwork became too heavy to stand up. The construction of a high-rise building begins with the foundation, which stops its huge weight from sinking into the ground. Next comes the structure of the building – its steel or concrete frame. Floors and walls are gradually added. Finally, windows and doors, lighting, plumbing, telephone lines, and so on are added. When everything is complete, people can move in.

SAFETY IS VERY important in high-rise buildings. The greatest danger is fire. If it starts on the lower floors, fire can spread very rapidly up through a building. So apartment buildings are built with fire-resistant materials that slow down the spread of the flames. Sets of doors called fire doors stop flames from racing along the corridors inside the building. It is important that these doors stay closed. Smoke detectors automatically set off water sprinklers to put out the fire. If there is a fire, people have to use either emergency exit routes or fire escapes to reach the ground level.

27

A Model
APARTMENT
BUILDING

An apartment building consists of several floors on top of each other. On the bottom level there might be parking spaces, waste disposal areas, heating boilers, electrical substations, and other services. Each floor usually has the same layout of apartments and corridors. An area on each floor is taken up by the stairs and elevators. You can make a model building with these features.

To make a model apartment building
You may need:

- **thick cardboard or plywood baseboard (about 8 in x 12 in/20 cm x 30 cm)**
- **strips of wood**
- **thick cardboard**
- **thin cardboard**
- **popsicle sticks**
- **glue**
- **plastic wrap**

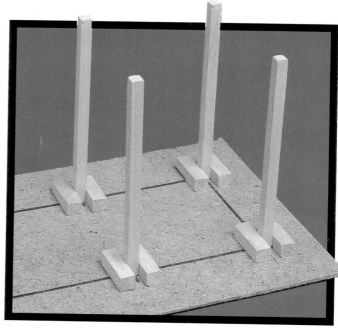

1 Draw a plan for each floor of your apartment building. Decide how many apartments you want on each floor, where the corridor to the front doors will be, and where to put the stairs. Also, decide how many floors you want and how high each one will be. Draw the ground-floor plan on the baseboard.

2 Now begin to build a frame. Cut six strips of wood for columns to support the floors. Glue the columns onto the baseboard. Use small blocks of wood around the columns to keep them upright. These are like the foundations of a real building.

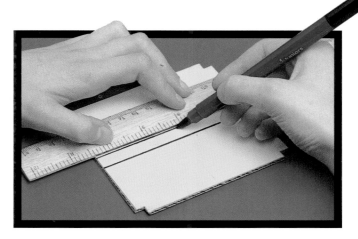

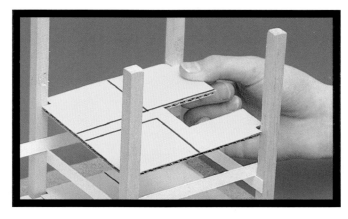

3 Cut pieces of cardboard for the floors. At each corner cut out a small square so that the floors fit around the columns. Draw the floor plan on each section of floor. Cut a hole in the first and second floors for the stairs.

4 Glue popsicle sticks or strips of paper or wood between the columns at each floor level. These will stiffen the frame and support the floors. Put the floor sections in place.

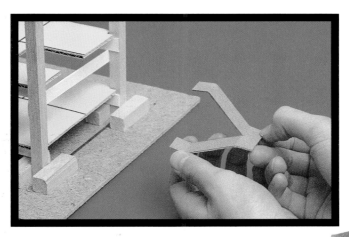

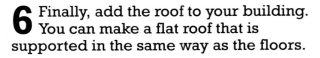

5 Cut sets of stairs out of thick cardboard. Glue them in place between the floors. Use thin cardboard to make walls for the corridors and walls between the apartments.

6 Finally, add the roof to your building. You can make a flat roof that is supported in the same way as the floors.

Did You Know...
... that one of the most important inventions for tall buildings was the elevator? A steam-powered elevator was built by Elisha Otis in the 1850s. The first electric elevators were installed in buildings in the late 1880s.

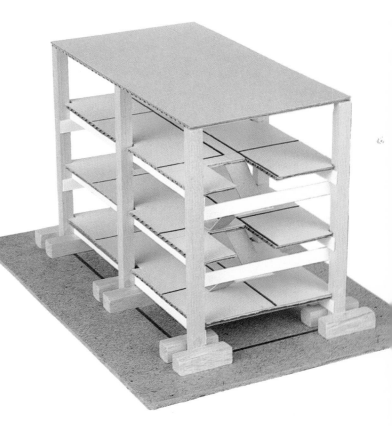

Add the outside wall to the building. Make windows from plastic wrap. Also add walls for an elevator shaft next to the stairs. What about a fire escape?

Can you add a parking lot and flower beds outside the building?

GLOSSARY

Beam
A horizontal section of the frame in a building. A beam is suppported at each end.

Cavity wall
A wall that has two layers of bricks with a space in between. Cavity walls help to stop heat from escaping out of a house and dampness from coming into it.

Collector
A device that traps the sun's energy and uses it to heat water or air.

Column
A vertical section of the frame in a building. Columns carry the weight of the building down to the ground level.

Curtain wall
The outer wall of a castle.

Daub
Mud or clay that is added onto wattle to make a solid wall.

Double glazing
A glass window or door that has two panes of glass separated by a small gap. Double glazing helps to stop heat from escaping.

Felt
A fabric that is made by pressing together woolen fibers.

Foundation
The solid base on top of which a building stands. A foundation spreads the weight of a building over the ground.

Glass fiber
A very thin thread of glass. Glass fibers can be made into insulating material.

Insulation
Material that is used to slow down the loss of heat from buildings. It traps the warm air inside the building.

Keep
The main tower of a castle.

Monsoon
A strong wind that blows across southern Asia and often brings heavy rains.

Nomad
A person who moves from one place to another, usually with a group of people. Nomads wander in search of food, or water, or pasture for their animals.

Plaster
A mixture of sand, lime, and water. It is used to make a smooth coating for walls.

Solar
Describes anything to do with the sun.

Sprinkler
A device that sprays water over a wide area. Sprinklers are often part of the automatic fire-fighting system in large public buildings.

Synthetic
A material, such as nylon, that is not natural.

Tenement
A building that is divided up into separate apartments. People who live in them often share bathing and cooking facilities.

Thatch
A roofing material made from bundles of straw or reed.

Wattle
A wall that is made by weaving branches together.

RESOURCES

Materials
Most of the items used in the projects in this book can be obtained from craft shops, artists' supply stores, or home improvement centers.

Places to visit
Arlington Heights Historical Museum
110 W. Fremont Street
Arlington Heights, IL 60004
Tel: (708) 255-1225

Bacon's Castle
Route 10
Surry County, VA 23883
Tel: (804) 866-8483

Colonial Williamsburg
Williamsburg, VA 23185
Tel: (804) 229-1000

The Gardner Museum of Architecture & Design
332 Maine Street
Quincy, IL 62301
Tel: (217) 224-6873

Lumbertown USA
Madens Resort, Gull Lake
Brainerd, MN 56401
Tel: (218) 829-8872

Sioux Lookout D.A.R. Log Cabin Museum
E. 4th and Memorial Park
North Platte, NE 69101
Tel: (308) 532-0571

Swiss Historical Village
6th Avenue and 7th Street
New Glarus, WI 53574
Tel: (608) 527-2317

Tappantown Historical Society
Tappan, NY 10983
Tel: (914) 359-2361

Troy Museum and Historic Village
60 W. Wattles Road,
Troy, MI 48098
Tel: (313) 524-3570

Books to read
Building Homes by Graham Rickard (Lerner), 1989.
Building Technology by Mark Lambert (Bookwright), 1991.
High-Rise by Richard Younker (Crowell Jr.), 1980.
Houses and Homes by Alistair Hamilton MacLaren (Bookwright), 1992.
Spiderwebs to Skyscrapers: The Science of Structures by David Darling (Dillon), 1991.
Stone, Clay, Glass: How Building Materials Are Found and Used by Robert L. Bates (Enslow), 1987.

INDEX

Additional photographs:
Robert Harding Picture Library 7
(Linda Proud), 10, 18 (Adam Woolfitt),
27; ZEFA Picture Library 14.